A Model A

Leilanie Stewart
A Model Archaeologist

20/20 **EYEWEAR**
PAMPHLET SERIES
2015

First published in 2015 by Eyewear Publishing Ltd
74 Leith Mansions, Grantully Road
London W9 1LJ United Kingdom

Typeset with graphic design by Edwin Smet
Printed in England by Lightning Source
All rights reserved © 2015 *Leilanie Stewart*
The right of Leilanie Stewart to be identified as author
of this work has been asserted in accordance with section 77
of the Copyright, Designs and Patents Act 1988

ISBN 978-1-908998-68-2
WWW.EYEWEARPUBLISHING.COM

*Thanks are due to
Todd Swift and Eyewear for their dedication and commitment
to my poetry, to Ken W Simpson for his professional support and to
Joseph Robert, my husband, fellow poet and artist of life.*

*It is the creative ability
of a human being that separates him
from all other animals.*
Bruce Lee, Striking Thoughts

Table of contents

- 9 A Model Archaeologist
- 10 Warfare
- 12 Personification
- 14 Hadrian's Wall
- 16 Peat Bog
- 17 Tour Guide
- 18 Fieldwork
- 19 Kleenex Ad
- 20 Spoil Heap
- 21 Bullocks
- 22 Bondage
- 24 Bronze Dagger
- 25 Retouch
- 26 Impressions of an Archaeologist
- 27 Clay Tablet
- 28 Belemnite Soup
- 29 Sandland
- 30 The Hole of Truth
- 31 Idle
- 32 Nautical Almanac

- 35 Acknowledgements

A Model Archaeologist

My tutor and my classmates
said I was the glamour girl of archaeology
when a modelling photo of me appeared
in the *Belfast Telegraph*, with a blurb below.

I told them it was a fun job to do
that helped pay my university fees
I suppose I'm the Gertrude Bell type;
not just a pretty face.

I can swing my five pound mattock all day
and shovel the dirt in my trench, no problem
I'll happily be a Jill-of-all-trades.
I'll be a model. An archaeologist. Tough. I'll be me.

Warfare

I've never been much impressed
by swords and daggers,
bows and arrows
when I go to a museum
and to be honest,
I didn't give it much thought
until a guest brought
crossbows and longbows
into a tutorial.

I can't speak for all women,
but I wondered
if it was a girl thing;
not to care too much for warfare
though I admit, I was surprised
to find out that longbows
are much more deadly
than crossbows
and shoot much further.

I guess it makes sense
that a crossbow shoots faster
and more powerfully
at closer range,
but longbows were more deadly
in a war,
piercing shields,
tearing through armour
like paper.

And I was shocked to find out
that the Amazon women
who were trained
to use bows from birth
cut off one breast
so that they could perfect their aim
by pulling their arm back
across a flat chest.
It really just goes to show,

I can't speak for women at all.

Personification

The lecture theatre was darkened
and I sat, half asleep,
as we watched a DVD,
my late night of boozing
finally
getting the better of me,
and just as my eyelids
began to droop,
it caught my attention:
a statue of Boudica
on her chariot
storming
through the Roman towns
seeking retaliation
for the rape of her two daughters
by Roman soldiers.

It's easy to dehumanise
stories of ancient times,
dismissing them as having
no significance in present day life;
a detached reality,
though there is no separation
and the problems with society
never change.
And I, as a woman
in her early twenties
took a small piece
of barbaric history,
so that I could finally identify
with the past

sympathise
empathise
realise the truth

Hadrian's Wall

It was a Saturday afternoon
and I stood in a shopping centre
in the middle of Belfast
in a slinky dress
handing out goody bags
for a department store
with a beautiful
South African model
in my agency.

A man approached,
more interested in us
than the products we promoted
and he told me, in a jovial way,
that a girl like me
should be off to college
instead of parading herself
like a show horse.

Patronizing, of course,
but I knew he meant well
so I told him about my uni course
aside from my part-time income.
He was giddy then,
and mentioned
his amateur interest
in the Roman occupation of Britain.

He said he had something
that might help with my course,
and came back later on
with a book on Hadrian's Wall.

I gave him a goody bag for his wife
and took the book, thinking,
that Hadrian's Wall had been built
to keep people apart, but this time

it had bridged a gap.

Peat Bog

It seems counterintuitive to me,
to wipe your dirty hands
after excavating
on the fern that grows on a peat bog
but it's perfectly hygienic;
you can eat your food
and not get ill.

Not so my professor's dog,
that apparently ate
some Bronze Age butter
found in a wooden urn
thrown into a long-gone lake
as an offering to pagan gods,
now perfectly preserved
in the anaerobic soil.

The dog ate the butter
that was drying out
on the hood of the professor's car
and the poor creature
got violently ill.

Peat bogs may be cleaner
than we imagine,
but the milk produce
of cows that are 4000 years dead
and preserved inside it, isn't.

Tour Guide

Nine months before I graduated,
the ideal job came up;
a tour guide and curator
in Bangor museum.

I'd always thought about a job
that balanced the solitary work
of handling artefacts
with social interaction.

My tutor suggested that I could link
modelling and archaeology
by becoming a tour guide;
an educated, but pretty face.

The job was gone before I left Queens
and, like the cancellation
of free grants the year before me
my generation lost out.

The seventies kids
sailed the last of the easy ride,
before the Ice Age
came in the eighties;

bringing the permafrost
of economic decline,
to settle on the tundra
of fresh graduates.

Fieldwork

Two months into my first dig,
I kneeled in my trench
on my foam pad,
set down my trowel
to rub my tired knuckles
and stood up to stretch
my stiff knees.

Archaeologists often retire
with arthritis
one of the pitfalls of the job.

I thought then,
how long would it take
between handing out goody bags
in skimpy clothes
and trowelling earth and clay
in all weather
for nature to finally get
the better of my bones.

Kleenex Ad

Can you imagine,
spending all day
in the archaeological
head office basement
scrubbing cow teeth
and sheep mandibles
with a toothbrush,
laying them out to dry,
painting tippex on them,
giving them numerical codes

Then trowelling on
a quick-fix of makeup,
lathering on foundation
thick like winter varves
taking off overalls,
slipping on stilettos
and an eye-catching dress
to audition for a TV Ad:

I had to play a jilted bride,
crying at the altar,
as a priest gave a tissue,
then throw a pretend bouquet
at my imaginary husband

I didn't get the job:
maybe they knew that
I'd be better off using Kleenex
to wipe the soil off my face,
or maybe it was my calloused hands,
much too rough for a bride-to-be.

Spoil Heap

The director said if we found
any artefacts accidently thrown
onto the spoil heap by a digger,

we could pocket them. It didn't matter,
since they weren't found in situ
and therefore couldn't be

dated. So in this way, I built up
my own little collection of thumbnail
scrapers, shell-shaped tools

once used by someone
to clean sinew and hair
off animal skins, but now,

they're in my own private
Tupperware museum;
for me to wonder who

made them, used them,
tossed them away
by a riverside, or into a fire.

Bullocks

The Bronze Age site
where I worked, one summer
was next to a field.

And one day, someone left
the gate open, so that
five bullocks escaped.

They ran amok on our site,
but when we tried to catch them,
they were too fast.

That day, we'd laid out
intact pottery bowls
to dry in the sun.

The bullocks trampled them
all to pieces, and I thought,
it was a damn shame.

Immaculate, held in the clay
for four millennia, only to be
destroyed, and us with no reward.

Bondage

I got my waist-length hair
cut short
as it got in the way
of my work on site,
blowing in my face
in windy weather,
and sticking to my neck
on a hot day.

My agent was angry.
Naturally,
she liked it long
for the hair-shoots I did,
so she got me a job
suited to my new cropped look:
modelling bondage gear.

I had to wear
a £300 leather-basque,
and skin-tight black trousers,
wearing huge false eyelashes
and theatrical makeup
to show well in sepia prints,
for a dominatrix-catalogue.
Fun.

The photographer quivered
with excitement, at my
fieldwork-toned biceps,
and he got me to pull back
my shoulders, with my hands
on my hips, to highlight my arms
together with my slicked-back hair.

Digging, and shovelling
and carrying heavy buckets
of soil all day
gives an archaeologist muscles.
But we like to joke that our biceps
are due to a pint at the pub,
after long days on site.
We call this, in the trade,
the Archaeologist's curl.

Bronze Dagger

A guest speaker once came into
my tutorial and showed us a box
of bronze and iron daggers and swords.

He passed them around the room
telling the story behind each one and
emphasising how sharp they still were.

I scoffed — how could such rusted things;
implements that seemed so blunt,
even cut something like butter.

As if to prove my point,
subconsciously (perhaps),
I ran my finger along a dagger blade.

The blood flowed freely,
dotting the table, and more importantly,
dotting my mind.

I had a renewed respect for the dead;
those warriors who had perfected their tools,
to cut crude matter from the ethereal flow.

Retouch

I was offered bikini work
thanks to my golden tan
from summer excavations,
the swimwear a shoot
for stock photos.

Funny then,
that under the golden sheen
it was the first time
I'd felt self-conscious
on a job.

The very same dig
that had bestowed on me
the sun-kissed look
to get the work
had also left me bruised.

I posed anyway,
and was thankful, after
to see that they retouched
the purple splodges
on my knees from digging.

Impressions of an Archaeologist

You look too pretty
to be an archaeologist
And aren't you too young?
Do you find gold?
Do you have Indiana Jones
as your ring-tone?
Do you watch Time Team?
Do you dig in Egypt?
How many dinosaur bones
have you found?
Isn't it fun to design
your own building?
Oh wait,
that's architecture,
I see… archaeology
Finding treasure in tombs
Cool.

Clay Tablet

One day
I intend to write a poem
on a clay tablet

I figure
this is the only ticket to eternity
that a human will ever have

Even if
the world falls apart, my poem,
on its clay tablet, will last

Burn it
and it will be sealed forever,
fire-glazed

Technology will fail
yet my poem will live for eons
under the rubble

I'll make sure
to write something crude, lairy,
simply to offend the future generations

Ice can come and go
but the drumlins won't wipe me out
my tablet will be waiting

For someone,
or something, to dig it out,
fuss over it, then probably throw it

onto a spoil heap.

Belemnite Soup

I was swimming once
in a dream
in a tepid lake
There were two of me then
and one dissolved
into the limestone quarry
I watched the shale flake off
and all around
the pieces fell
They tumbled
into the pool
as the outer me melted
I was one
with the water;
a compound soup
I lost a part of myself
to the eons
of earth before me
I'd been in the lake once before
and I knew I'd never be there again
Drifting together once more
in the flow, I realised
I was free.

Sandland

The whiskey burns the throat
like sand in a storm over wasting dunes
and the spiky grass stands to attention
it stands and sways and is shot down
the aggregates are bullets on the breeze

It's a rough old life in Sandland
In Sandland they fall and are forgotten

But the whiskey has lost its medicine
and at night the ears crack
with the bangs and the cries
the roots go deep, but still sand erodes
it can't hold together under assault

It's a rough old life in Sandland
In Sandland they fall, though we try to remember.

The Hole of Truth

What's behind the ferns?
With their five pointed hands
and the dense jungle mists
of yesteryear

Through the grey pencil lines
that depress the thick foam
I can see past the leaves
between five points

What's behind the ferns?
Through the veins of the leaves
past the cracked plaster board
and the finger marks

Idle

Brain to glutes.
Twitch. Move.
Don't wanna

Don't need to

And to my head?
My fibula
fibuling

Brain to finger
a flicker
a tricker

It started there…

Leg over
Leg over
the willing, but

a moment
surrendered
thought lost in time.

Nautical Almanac

Watch me move my leguminous feet,
wriggle my toes into the earth
and see how the bacteria fix

nitrogen

which travels on a tidal surge
from nodule of root to acetate heart
then transpires through my aquiline core

not far from where I am.

Acknowledgements

I acknowledge the editors of the following publications in which some of these poems have appeared: *Inclement, Erbacce, Weyfarers, Sarasvati* and *The Journal*.

EYEWEAR PUBLISHING

EYEWEAR PAMPHLET SERIES

BEN STAINTON EDIBLES
MEL PRYOR DRAWN ON WATER
MICHAEL BROWN UNDERSONG
MATT HOWARD THE ORGAN BOX
RACHAEL M NICHOLAS SOMEWHERE NEAR IN THE DARK
BETH TICHBORNE HUNGRY FOR AIR
GALE BURNS OPAL EYE
PIOTR FLORCZYK BAREFOOT
LEILANIE STEWART A MODEL ARCHAEOLOGIST
SHELLEY ROCHE-JACQUES RIPENING DARK
SAMANTHA JACKSON SMALL CRIES

EYEWEAR POETRY

MORGAN HARLOW MIDWEST RITUAL BURNING
KATE NOAKES CAPE TOWN
RICHARD LAMBERT NIGHT JOURNEY
SIMON JARVIS EIGHTEEN POEMS
ELSPETH SMITH DANGEROUS CAKES
CALEB KLACES BOTTLED AIR
GEORGE ELLIOTT CLARKE ILLICIT SONNETS
HANS VAN DE WAARSENBURG THE PAST IS NEVER DEAD
DAVID SHOOK OUR OBSIDIAN TONGUES
BARBARA MARSH TO THE BONEYARD
MARIELA GRIFFOR THE PSYCHIATRIST
DON SHARE UNION
SHEILA HILLIER HOTEL MOONMILK
FLOYD SKLOOT CLOSE READING
PENNY BOXALL SHIP OF THE LINE
MANDY KAHN MATH, HEAVEN, TIME
MARION MCCREADY TREE LANGUAGE
RUFO QUINTAVALLE WEATHER DERIVATIVES
SJ FOWLER THE ROTTWEILER'S GUIDE TO THE DOG OWNER
TEDI LÓPEZ MILLS DEATH ON RUA AUGUSTA
AGNIESZKA STUDZINSKA WHAT THINGS ARE
JEMMA BORG THE ILLUMINATED WORLD
KEIRAN GODDARD FOR THE CHORUS
COLETTE SENSIER SKINLESS

EYEWEAR PROSE

SUMIA SUKKAR THE BOY FROM ALEPPO WHO PAINTED THE WAR
ALFRED CORN MIRANDA'S BOOK

EYEWEAR LITERARY CRITICISM

MARK FORD THIS DIALOGUE OF ONE

Lightning Source UK Ltd.
Milton Keynes UK
UKOW06f0013290515

252521UK00008B/108/P

9 781908 998682